Fluid Art Mastery

8 Steps To Being A Paint Pouring Artist

By Rick Cheadle

CHEADLE DESIGNS

About Rick Cheadle

Rick Cheadle is a self-taught mixed-media and

abstract artist, based in Davison, Michigan.

He draws inspiration for his varied creations

from Mid-Century art and design,

including abstract expressionism.

His portfolio includes large scale wall art pieces,

wall sculptures, found objects mobiles,

as well as a plethora of mixed media and

fine-art works.

Using his natural sensitivity to

color harmony and his keen attention

to detail, Cheadle creates a variety

of custom pieces in demand for

homes and businesses across the U.S. and Canada.

Other Books by Rick Cheadle:

Daily Journal and Goal Setting: Happy Life Quest:
An Inspired Life Through Journaling

Reselling: The Art of Flipping Art:
Buying and Selling Art for Huge Profits

Photography Made Easy:
The Beginners Guide To Learning Digital
Photography In A Weekend

Abstract Floral Designs:
Meditative Coloring for Stress Relief and Fun

Zen Time Colorscapes

Fluid Art Mastery:
8 Steps to Being a Paint Pouring Artist
Copyright© 2017 by Rick Cheadle

Legal Disclaimer:
This book contains strategies and tips and other
artistic advice that, regardless of my own
experiences and results, may not produce the same
results for you. Consequently, I make
no guarantees regarding results you achieve.
You assume sole responsibility for the
outcome of any application of information
provided in this book.

ISBN: 9781549657764

Foreward

Who is Rick Cheadle?
When I began searching the Internet for articles,tutorials
and videos on the subject of poured acrylic paintings,
Rick's name kept popping up among the dozens
of others, all artists making names for themselves with
this interesting art form. It took a while for me to
start watching his videos, because I was attracted to those
where the artist talks throughout the process.
Rick doesn't talk much; at least, not in his videos.
He teaches, by placing instructive text at
strategic locations in his videos, and by personally
demonstrating his techniques. The majority of other
artists' videos showed how to mix, layer, then pour the paints
onto various substrates but didn't address how to obtain
Consistent results in their desire for "cells,"
which many of us beginners struggled with.
As if reading our minds, Rick posted the outcome
of his experiments with the different
ingredients used to create the mixtures
that result in the almost-magical formation
of cells, every time.Rick, a successful self-taught artist with

years of experience, knows the professional-grade art supplies he prefers are expensive, perhaps out of the price-range for some beginners. To make this art form accessible to all, he began experimenting with house paints inexpensive craft paints one can find at big-box hobby and "dollar" stores, letting his viewers know which worked, or didn't. An essential ingredient in creating cells in this painting method is a dispersant, something that will cause the layered paints to rise to the surface and break into circles within circles of color. The body weight, or viscosity, of the layered paints determines which colors rise to the top quickest, a process that needs a flow medium. A flow medium thins the paints without changing the strength of the colors. Rick tested all sorts of dispersants and mediums in his search for reliable substitutes for more costly materials.

Rick Cheadle's passion for art and his drive to spread that passion to others, his curiosity about how things work the way they do and desire for answers, his inventiveness and strong entrepreneurial spirit all work to our benefit, helping us become the artists we dream of being.

To answer the question posed at the beginning of this introduction, I think Rick Cheadle is a modern renaissance person: artist, musician, writer, inventor, and generous teacher.

M. C. McLemore
Pennsylvania, USA
July, 2017

Dear Reader,

Thank you for purchasing my book,
Fluid Art Mastery:
8 Steps to Being a Paint Pouring Pro.

I believe the means of making art should be accessible
to everyone, which is the guiding force behind writing
this book. Poured fluid art is not a new idea, but the
materials and techniques have been changed
and adapted to meet the needs and methods of
today's artists. I believe you will enjoy the process
of poured painting and will be amazed at
the results you can achieve.

This book outlines the steps I take when producing
my poured acrylic paintings.
I will share with you how I set up my studio, the
materials I use in creating my art, and various
techniques I employ in bringing them to a finished state.
My book is meant to be a guide to help you learn
what to do and, more importantly, what *not* to do.

By following the techniques outlined in this book, you will
have enough knowledge to start making poured paintings of
your own. As you know, nobody can guarantee your success in
this field, but the methods revealed in this book will work for
you if you apply them correctly. That's my promise.

So, are you ready? Great! Let's get started.
Happy Pouring!

Rick Cheadle

Table of Contents

Step 1
A Very Brief History Of Fluid Art

David Alfaro Siqueiros
(December 29, 1896, - January 6, 1974)
Mexican muralist; conceived a style of painting in
the 1930s referred to as an *accidental painting,*
in which he was able to create a variety of
unexpected shapes and textures.
He did this by layering different paints
that had varying densities. Siqueiros introduced
the use of non-traditional art materials
(commercial art paints, industrial paints)
and techniques (using industrial paint sprayers,
house paint brushes, spilled paint) and substrates
(sides of commercial buildings, for example)
to create his art. He was an early influence on
American abstract artist, Jackson Pollack.

*"The artist must paint as he would speak. I don't want people
to speculate what I mean, I want them to understand"
-David Alfaro Siqueiros*

Paul Jenkins (July 12, 1923 – June 9, 2012)

American Abstract Expressionist started paint pouring
in the late 1950s. Paul Jenkins was an influential artist
in the New York School. He was a huge presence in the
cultivation of abstract expressionism. I was fortunate
enough to own one of his paintings (since sold), titled
"Phenomena Jade Winds Walking."
He has been my major source of inspiration in
my paint pouring art.

*"I try to paint like a crapshooter throwing dice, utilizing past
experience and my knowledge of the odds,
it's a big gamble, and that's why I love it."
- Paul Jenkins*

This is the first painting I owned by Paul Jenkins,
"Phenomena - Jade Winds Walking,"
on a 6' x 10' canvas in 1977,
pictured here in my dining room.
The canvas was so large I had to rent a U-Haul
to transport it!

Paul Jenkins often painted on large canvases
like this. His dirty-pour "cups" often
were made in full-size trash cans!

Set Up Your Studio

First We Must Talk Safety!

There are hazards involved with anything in life and most problems can be avoided with a little knowledge and common sense. This is also true when creating art.

Most products you purchase for your paint pouring endeavor will include instructions and safety recommendations. **Read the SDS (Safety Data Sheet)**. Read and follow these thoroughly.

Always use caution when using anything caustic and when using any type of flame.
Be careful not to burn your canvas, paint or working area. Off-gassing (the release of volatile organic compounds [VOCs] or other chemicals) is also hazardous. The silicone and all the stuff used in paint pouring wasn't made to be heated up.
Use caution!
Always work in a well-ventilated area.

Workplace Essentials Include the following:
Safety glasses
Protective clothing
Latex gloves
Respirator
C_1O (carbon monoxide) alarm
Fire extinguisher

Ok, now let's prep your studio.

You can get as fancy and elaborate as you want with your work space and tools. I have listed most of the items that I use or have used. You could pick one item or all the items in each category. Remember, these are just recommendations. You will start getting the feel for things and customize your paint pouring toolkit to your own personal style.

An Overhead View of my Work Space

Work Surface

Sturdy and level table

Drop cloth, plastic sheeting or shower liner works

A shallow tub or bin with a lip (to catch paint run-off)

A rack to place your substrate on for painting

Or

Inexpensive paint pouring set ups. The photo on the left is a wire rack that is flipped upside down. Total cost $6. Or an even more inexpensive option is pictured on the right. It consists of two types of aluminum pans.

Total cost $2.

I use the setups below when I do paint pouring clinics.

Two Easy "Starter" Work Space Options

Aluminium Roaster Pan and Casserole Pan

Paints

Inexpensive craft paints

Latex house paint (flat)

Student-grade acrylic paints

Soft-bodied acrylic paints

Heavy-bodied acrylic paints

Fluid acrylics

High-Flow acrylics

Inks

And More

Mediums and Alternatives

Pouring Mediums (Liquitex ™ Pouring Medium)

PVA/Elmer's ™ Glue (non-archival)

PVAc/Bookbinder's Glue (archival)

Floetrol ™ (flow aid)

Glazing Mediums

Gloss Mediums

Airbrush Medium

And More

Substrates*

Canvas (including recycled canvases)

Wood panel/ hardboard/Easy Flow™ Panels

Wood panel/ hardboard cradled

Yupo® paper

Mixed media paper

Old CD's

Old record albums

Ceramic tiles

Rocks and stones

Old windows

Furniture

And More

(*__Please note:__ Regardless what substrate you choose to paint on, I recommend at least two coats of gesso or paint primer be applied [and allowed to dry] prior to any paint pouring. Also, depending on how you want your piece to look, white primer base coat will make your art brighter and a black primer base coat will make your colors richer.)

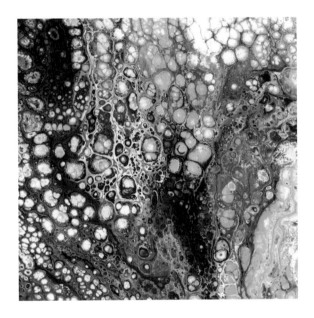

"Strident" by Rick Cheadle

Other Materials

Pouring Cups—5-ounce cups (or larger)
for individual colors
9-ounce cups (or larger) for dirty pours

Jumbo Craft Sticks

Optional Additives (to aid in "cell" creation.)
More research is required to test their archival quality.
Silicone spray
Auto Lubricant
Hair Products that contain dimethicone

Heat Source (embossing tool, heat gun or
butane torch)

Plastic condiment bottles with caps

Painting Knife / Spatula / Knock down knife
(for wide path swiping)

Trowels (for skimming and making designs in
the paint)

Pipettes (for adding small amounts of
water to mix)

Paper towels, apron and gloves

...and one more thing:

A journal.

Keep an Art Journal

Writing while creating clarifies and
focuses our minds.
Every time we try something new, make a new
discovery or totally ruin a new canvas, it is all part
of the journey and keeping track of your wins
and losses is also part of the journey.

Before I videotaped my art sessions,
I kept a journal of everything that worked
and what didn't. Now that I tape everything,
I don't make as frequent journal entries
but I still do it!

Prepare Your Paints

Mixing Ratio Essentials

The consistency of all of your paints is the essential

element in assuring a successful pour.

The ways of achieving the ideal consistency

vary quite a bit from one artist to another.

You may find that another artist's "recipe"

suits you better.   By all means search until

you get the results you are looking for,

and are happy with the outcome.

In this book, I will show you how I personally achieve
the proper fluidity that gives consistent results for me,
for students in my classes and countless other
paint-pouring enthusiasts that I hear from daily.

I recently released a video of an experiment where
I spent, basically, ten dollars at a dollar store on
paints and utilized my "mixology," and had
amazing results. Give my "budget" mix a chance.
It is easy to do and it doesn't cost much money.

I like to keep things simple, especially when learning something new. My recommendation is to find one mix (recipe) and develop your concoction around that. (Over time I have developed an intuitive sense of how things work together; I don't measure or weigh anything anymore. Mixing and stirring each individual color takes long enough, I certainly don't want to add more steps and time into that process.)

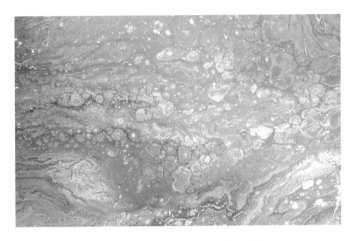

"Liquid" 2017 by Rick Cheadle

Making Sense Of Pouring Mediums and Additives In Relation To Acrylic Paints in Fluid Art/Paint Pours

Pouring Medium = The vehicle by which the color/paint is delivered

Liquitex Pouring Medium
GOLDEN GAC800
Lineco Bookbinders Glue

Elmer's Glue
Mod Podge
Floetrol

Acrylic Paints = The passengers of the vehicle

Additives = Luggage along for the ride.

Silicone   Dimethicone   Isopropyl Alcohol

Destination = Substrate

Art Panel   Tile   Record Album   Canvas

My Mixology:

Fine Art Mix *(archival)* 9 oz. Of Liquitex®
Pouring Medium, 2 oz. Gloss Medium, 2 oz.
Floetrol®, 4 ounces of alkaline water and
1 ounce of GOLDEN® GAC800.
Then add paint. The amount of paint
depends on the paint type, opacity and density.
(optional - add a few drops of alcohol, silicone
or dimethicone prior to pouring and lightly stir.)

Budget Mix (Elmer's® School Glue™/PVA) *(non-
archival)*—1 part acrylic paint to 1 part
PVA, mix well; add water to reach desired
consistency. (optional - add a few drops of
alcohol, silicone or dimethicone prior
to pouring and lightly stir.)

Budget Mix (Elmer's® Glue-All™)
(non-archival) - ¼ cup (2 fl. ounces) acrylic paint
to ¾ cup (6 fl. ounces) Glue-All™ mix*.
(optional - add a few drops of alcohol, silicone
or dimethicone prior to pouring and lightly stir.)

(*Glue-All™ —I mix ¾ cup glue to ¼ cup water.)

Floetrol® Mix 1 part Floetrol® with 4 parts highly-
pigmented fluid acrylics,
or 1 part Floetrol® with 2 parts heavy-body
acrylic paints. (optional - add a few drops
of alcohol, silicone or dimethicone prior
to pouring and lightly stir.)

One size does not fit all!

There are many variables to consider when
following a paint pour "recipe":

Climate (temperature/humidity)

Paint brands

Paint types (fluid, soft body, house
paint, etc.)

Paint opacity

Water used (different PH levels,
distilled, tap water)

Water temperature

Types and brands of additives used
(pouring medium, PVA, bookbinder's
glue, silicones, dimethicone etc.)

I recommend all artists to experiment, takes notes
(I keep a journal in my studio)
and figure out what works for you,
and what doesn't.

A Word About Cell Creation

One of the most frequent questions I receive is
"How do I make cells?"
My longstanding opinion is that it's all about the
fluidity of each individual color and
how they react with each other.
This is what I have found to be
fundamental in cell creation.

But! Acrylic paint colors and their relative
densities are also important. When I am creating
a pour I am thinking in terms of,
"How do I make the light layers break away from
the darker colors and help them rise up and
through to create 'cells'?"
If you have the consistencies correct, and you
understand the paints' densities and
how they react with each other, it's a
beautiful thing to watch the cells form,
almost as if by magic.

Silicone and alcohol do make a difference
but they are not a requirement for cell creation.

"Gluidance" 2017 By Rick Cheadle

The chart on the next page is a helpful guide
I use for reference. The paints in this chart are
the acrylic paints that come in tubes,
not the high-flow type of paints.
All brands have varying densities,
so I recommend experimenting and
making your own chart based on the paints
that you use. This is a non-scientific guide
so there is no guarantee of its accuracy.

Acrylic Paint Density

Pigment / Color — (from thinnest to heaviest)

Pigment / Color	
Fluorescent Colors	
Quinacridone Violet	
Quinacridone Magenta	more transparent
Nickel Azo Yellow	
Quinacridone Red	
Phthalo Green	
Ultramarine Blue	
Ultramarine Violet	
Burnt Sienna	
Burnt Umber	neutrals
Raw Sienna	
Cobalt Blue	
Raw Umber	
Cadmium Yellow	
Mars Black	
Cerulean Blue Deep	
Cobalt Turquoise	more opaque
Cadmium Red Dark	
Cobalt Green	
Cadmium Orange	
Cadmium Red	
Titanium and Zinc White	

Opaque/Translucent/Transparent:
terms used to describe the way paint reacts to light.

Opaque
Opaque paints are heavier in density and don't allow light to go through. The light bounces back; you cannot see through opaque paints.

Translucent
Translucent paints are less dense than opaque paints and do transmit light, but the light is scattered as it goes through giving it a frosted appearance.

Transparent
Transparent paints are lightest in density and allow light to go through to layers beneath. It can appear almost clear as glass. An example of this is the clear varnish you apply to your painting after it has dried. Clear coatings do not alter the colors they cover.

Another example, paint colors listed as transparent that allow you to see the colors laid down first. A transparent paint layer will alter the look of the color underneath it. Yellow over blue will reflect green, for instance.

The following chart demonstrates the qualities of opaque, translucent and transparent.

Paint Opacity Comparison

Opaque   Translucent   Transparent

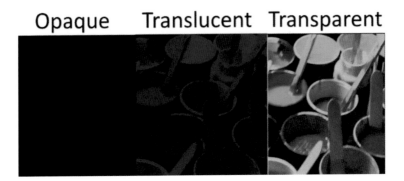

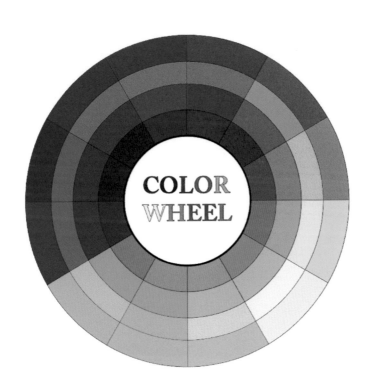

COLOR
WHEEL

Color Theory

First, The Color Wheel

I recommend for beginners to buy a color wheel.
Color wheels can be found online,
in art supply and book stores, among other places.
They are very handy to get a grasp of color
theory and why certain colors work
together and why others don't.
Using a color wheel will improve your color
selection for each painting,
will help you understand the concepts of balance
and harmony in creating art.
They explain the basics of color mixing and
relationships:
primary colors (red, yellow and blue),
pure colors which cannot be made by
mixing colors to get them;
secondary colors
(orange, green and purple/violet),
created by mixing two primaries together, and so.

Balance

Even though many times our paint pours
are considered random, it is possible—
and you are encouraged to try—to keep balance
in your work. That is why the way you tip the canvas,
the way you swipe, all play a roll in the
look of your piece.

Are the colors balanced?
Are the design elements flowing?
These are all things to consider
while manipulating your paint.

Harmony

Does everything in your artwork work together?
Is there "that one spot" you're just not happy with?

There are many aspects to consider: forms, spaces,
color harmony and the flow or rhythm, the movement
of the elements all play a factor in
a harmonious painting.

Remember, after your paint pour dries you
can add embellishments and bring it all together
and make it work. The pour doesn't have to be the
end of the story. A lot of times, in my case, it is
the beginning of the story.

Composition

When done correctly, a good composition
will draw your viewer in and keep their
eyes moving across the whole canvas.

Step 4

Know The Techniques

In poured painting, there is a variety of ways to
apply paint without using brushes or any other
traditional tools.
As mentioned in Chapter 1, Paul Jenkins
used trash cans to pour onto his canvases.
However, the techniques discussed in this
book are for paintings of a much smaller scale.
At some point in your fluid-art career,
the scale of the canvas you use might
dictate a larger cup, perhaps even a
half-gallon pitcher (!), but I recommend you
start off smaller until you can judge the
volume of paints and additives and the size
of tools a larger substrate requires.

Dirty Pour
Layers of paints poured on top of each other in
the same cup makes a "dirty pour" cup.
I try always to include white in every pour and
I usually begin my paint layering in the dirty pour
cup with Zinc or Titanium White.
I do this because white is the heaviest paint
and it sinks to the bottom once the cup
has been flipped on the canvas.
This causes many interesting effects
including lacing, webbing, and cells.
Familiarizing yourself with paint transparency
and opacity is helpful when deciding on
what order to pour your paints
into the dirty pour cup.

When I begin a dirty pour I usually start with white paint, adding a color or two, then I spray silicone in the cup; add more colors, add more white, and so on. I average around three squirts of silicone per dirty pour cup separated by at least 2-3 colors. I stir the dirty pour cup very little if at all. I don't stir too much because I want to maintain separation of the colors, not create muddy colors. Once you have all of your colors layered in a cup, you pour onto the substrate of choice (for the remainder of the book I will refer to as "canvas").
At this point, you can move the canvas to manipulate the paints.

Tipping the canvas allows paint to cover the whole surface (or nearly all of it), letting excess paint run over the edges.
This method gives the artwork a "flowing" appearance, very popular with many artists. There are numerous ways to manipulate the paint and get more design elements, like scraping, swiping and skimming, which I will cover later in this chapter.

Once the canvas is covered, I touch up the sides with the paint run-off. When I have complete coverage and I'm happy with the composition of the painting, I will introduce heat by using a chef's torch or a heat gun.
The heat is what helps generate cellular activity in the work. The oils from the additives react with the heat and create "cells."
Always use caution when heating up your art.
Please follow all of the safety recommendations discussed earlier in the book.

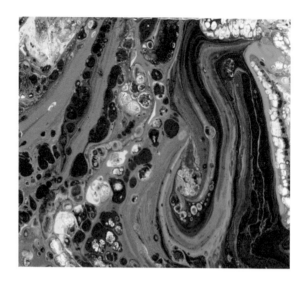

"Slink" by Rick Cheadle

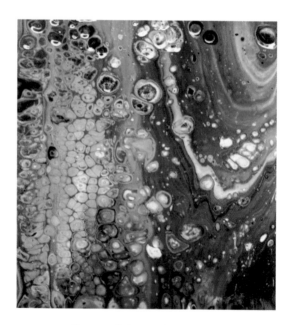

"Luxoril" by Rick Cheadle

Flip Cup

The flip cup is prepared exactly like a dirty pour
in terms of mixing and layering the paints into
one dirty pour. The flip cup technique is more
of a description of how you get the paint on the
surface of your canvas. In short, you flip it over.

While holding the dirty pour cup (which is sitting
on your work-space) with your left hand, pick up the
canvas with your right hand and place the canvas
face down over the cup opening. Then carefully pick
up both the cup and canvas (while holding the cup
tightly against the canvas), flip them over to where
now the canvas is on the workspace with the cup
sitting atop the canvas. I usually let the cup sit on the
canvas for 20-30 seconds to allow the dirty pour
contents to settle. Then with one motion,
I remove the cup from the canvas;
all the paint pours out and onto the canvas.

At this point, I move and tilt the canvas around
and get full canvas coverage. When the top is covered,
I touch up the sides of the canvas with the paint run-off.
Once the canvas is covered I touch up the sides with the
paint run off. When I have complete coverage, and I'm
happy with the composition of the painting, I will
introduce heat by using a chef's torch or a heat gun.

The heat is what helps generate cellular activity in
the work. The oils from the additives react with the heat,
rising up through the paint layers, creating the cells.
***Always* use caution when heating up your art!**
Please follow all of the safety recommendations
discussed earlier in the book.

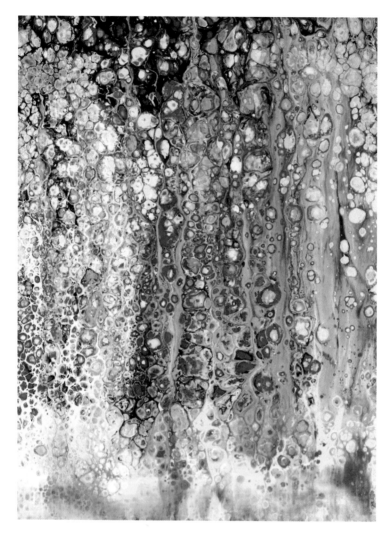

"Cascadian" by Rick Cheadle

A Few Variations on the Basic Techniques

The "Reserve" Flip Cup

Basically, the "Reserve" flip cup is prepared exactly
the same as a flip cup pour but instead of emptying
all of the paint on the canvas, you use a quick
motion when lifting to ensure saving some
of the dirty pour mixture at the bottom of the
cup to later cover corners and edges.

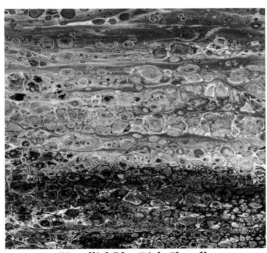
"Strullish" by Rick Cheadle

The Flip and Drag

This is a technique I sometimes use prior to lifting a
flip cup off the canvas. Basically, I flip the cup onto the
canvas. With the canvas sitting on the rack I simply
slide the cup around the surface of the canvas making
sure I get close to all four corners. My thought with this
is that it will help with the flow of the paint over the
edges and corners upon lifting the cup.

Puddle Pour

Puddle pours are a layering of color(s) on the
canvas in one or more puddles that allow the paint
to flow out and/or into each other. When there is
enough paint on the surface, the canvas can be tipped
and the colors will disperse and create designs
and unique color combinations throughout
the canvas depending on the degree of tilting.

A variation of this technique is a puddle pour with
void fill (a puddle pour with an added pour covering
the blank spots of the canvas). Once the canvas is
covered I touch up the sides with the paint run off.
When I have complete coverage and I'm happy with the
composition of the painting, I will introduce heat
by using a chef's torch or a heat gun.
The heat is what helps generate cellular
activity in the work.

**Again, *always* use caution
when heating up your art, and follow all of the safety
recommendations discussed earlier in the book.**

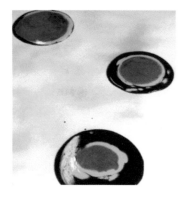

"puddle Pour"   "Puddle Pour" with void fill

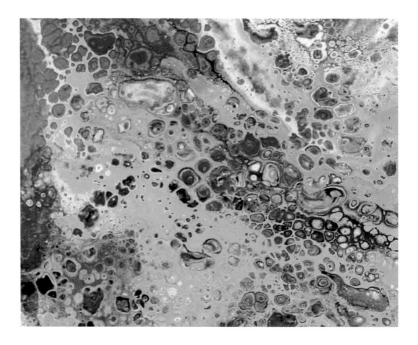

"Smidgy" by Rick Cheadle

Open Cylinder

This method employs a bottomless cup.
Artist Andy Drop was the first artist I saw using
this method. The idea here is to do a self-contained
dirty pour that isn't actually poured.
The bottomless cup or some other container is a
vessel that keeps the paints inside allowing for a
lot of unique possibilities and color combos once
the cup is lifted from the canvas. I like this type of
pour on small canvases but I mostly use
this method on extra-large canvases when
I need more precise color placement.

As with the previous techniques, once the canvas
is covered I touch up the sides with the paint run-off.
If I like what I see, I will apply heat, as described
previously, to facilitate the development of cells.

"Open Cylinder" Pour

Ribbon Pour

I like to use this technique at the end of the paint pouring session when I have several colors leftover from the day's pourings. Sometimes I've used as many as 12 colors in a ribbon pour!

Depending on how much paint I have and what size canvas I am using, I pour the mix directly on the canvas, or sometimes I pour a thin layer of Zinc White or Titanium White down first. When pouring the paint, I try to be loose, pouring in a free-flowing motion. I try making a taffy or ribbon appearance with the paints. **When doing these types of pours, keep the tipping of the canvas to a minimum.**

The Ribbon Pour Technique on Easy Flow™ Panel

Swipe Technique

I pick 3-5 colors for the background colors.
Mix them according to my "mixology" and put 1-2
squirts of silicone in each color. I pour the 3-5 colors
on the canvas in a striped pattern occasionally crossing
over each other but not too much. At this point,
I tip the canvas to spread all the paints out over the
canvas. Once I have the canvas covered in my
background colors, I introduce the swipe-over color.
I use either white or black to do the swipe over.
I make sure that the swiping color is slightly thinner
than the other paints. I do not add silicone
to the swiping colors.

I always start at the end of the canvas that
I like the least. I pour a strip of paint from corner to
corner approximately 1-3 inches wide depending on
the size of the canvas. (Another guide is to cover
10%- 20% of one end of the canvas.)
Then I take heavy card stock (or a 3-ml laminating
sheet or something similar) and begin swiping
the white paint over the initial layers that were poured.
I sometimes increase the white and repeat the
process over the whole canvas until I get the look
I'm trying to achieve.

Doing these swiping motions should generate
many cells when done correctly. Getting a feel
for the swipe is the key. You want to lightly skim
the heavy card stock or a 3-ml laminating sheet,
or something similar (even a paper bag), over the paints.
This takes practice but it is worth
the time to get this right.

"Swiping" with a paper bag

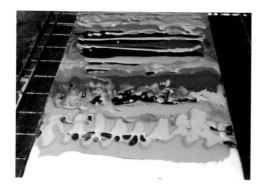

Example of paints laid out on canvas pre-swipe

Pictured is a large canvas ready for the swipe technique:
this canvas has 6 colors plus white. I normally only
use 3-5 colors but this piece was larger than
what I usually work with. Notice how the
white covers the bottom 10% of the canvas.
This is the "swipe over" color.

Swipe with knock down knife

Sometimes a pour doesn't go as planned, sometimes the colors run together and make "mud," or the colors aren't quite right—or I'm just not feeling it. Well, that's the time I break out the 'big gun'...the Knock-Down Knife. For this technique, I base my swiping color on what colors I will be swiping over. Example: If the colors are bright and cheerful I will swipe with black paint. If the colors are drab or muted I will swipe with white paint. I always think in terms of balance in my paintings. So, the way it works is: I pick my least favorite end of the canvas. I lay out my swiping paint (white, black or any color I decide on) and pour it directly on the poured canvas that I am swiping over from corner to corner. The amount of paint is approximately 1"- 3" in width depending on the size of the canvas. I then take the knock-down knife, and with a light touch, skim the top of the paint I just poured and pull it down the length of the canvas. This takes a lot of practice to get it right but once you get it down you'll love it. In fact, I have students that only use the swiping technique.

Multi-Swipe with Spatula

The way I usually do this type of swipe is as follows:
I pick 3-5 colors for the background colors.
Mix them according to my "mixology" and put
1-2 squirts of silicone in each color.
I pour the 3-5 colors all over the
canvas in a random fashion, occasionally
crossing over each other but not too much.
At this point, I tip the canvas to spread
all the paints out over the canvas.

Once I have the canvas covered in my background
colors I introduce the swipe-over color.
I use either white or black to do the swipe over.
I do not add silicone to either of these colors.
I always start at the end that I like the least and
pour a strip of paint from corner to corner
approximately 1-3-inches wide, depending on
the size of the canvas. Then, I take an art spatula
and begin swiping the white paint over the initial
paints that were poured. I sometimes add more
of the white paint, repeating the process over the
whole canvas until I get the look
I'm trying to achieve.

Doing these swiping motions should
generate many cells when done correctly.
Getting a feel for the swipe is the key.
You want to gently skim the spatula lightly
over the paints. This takes practice but
the time spent to get this right is not misspent.
I have saved many bad pours by
utilizing this technique.

"Jannocks" by Rick Cheadle

Multi-Layer

Begin with picking out your colors then start layering colors in various patterns on top of each other, keeping in mind not to pour too much paint on the surface (too much paint increases the chance of cracks to form). Once you have the whole canvas covered, you then pour either a single color or a dirty pour directly on the pre-poured canvas. I like to do this in a flowing swirling type pattern and just let the paint do its thing. Too much tipping and tilting of the canvas at this point will dissipate what you have created with the over-pour. However, if you are unhappy with the results of that added layer, you can tip the canvas and let the paint off and try again. **Or use my go-to solution when I'm just not happy with what I'm seeing: Swipe it!**

"Starzique" by Rick Cheadle

Dip and Swipe

This effect is accomplished using the run-off paint from previous pours. Dip the canvas into the collected puddles of paint, then using the swiping tool of your choice, perform one or multiple swipes until the desired result is achieved.

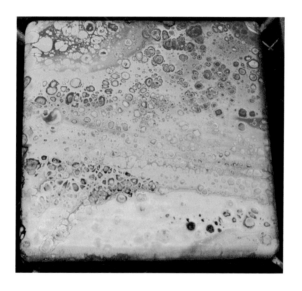

This is an example of a dip and swipe. Notice the black of the Easy Flow™ Panel coming through. This look was accomplished with two swipes of a drywall trowel.

Dip and Pour Over

Use the run-off paint from previous pours by dipping the canvas into the collected run-off paint, then using a dirty pour cup or a single-color cup. Pour directly on top of dipped canvas surface. From this point, you can tip, tilt and manipulate the paint into the desired look or you can also use swiping tools for an even more dramatic effect.

Canvas has been dipped into the paint run -off from previous pours then a new mix of color(s) are poured directly on top.

Dip, Pour and Swipe

Canvas dipped, poured-over then swiped.

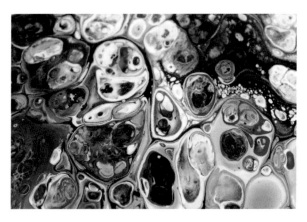

"Reshugah" 2017 by Rick Cheadle

was created using the "Dip, Pour and Swipe" method

Air Blown

For this technique, I pick out my colors and either pour single colors all over the canvas or combine in a dirty cup. The way I choose colors for these types of pours is usually I'll pick my favorite analogous color scheme (three adjacent colors on the color wheel*) for the first pour, then add three complimentary colors and blow on those three colors.

An example would be: base coat of yellow, yellow green and green poured all over and covering the canvas. Then using the complimentary color "red violet" I would pour puddles where ever I think it would look good keeping in mind basic design elements like composition and balance etc.

Once I have all of the colors poured onto the canvas surface, then I introduce air. I use a computer duster tube, but a straw works, or even an air compressor. The idea here is to blow air on to the canvas and manipulate the paints to create unique patterns and designs.

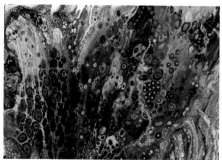

"Tressy" by Rick Cheadle

Dip and Peel

I sometimes use this technique when I have
too much leftover paint or a large accumulation
of paint run-off. Basically, you will load up a
canvas with the leftover paint OR
you can do this by pouring paints directly on
the canvas OR you can do a combination of both.
Ex: maybe you dipped your canvas into
the paint run-off and now you want to add a
complementary color on top of that.

Whatever method you choose to cover your
canvas will work. From that point,
you will set the painted canvas onto your work
station and with another prepped canvas, press
into the painted canvas making sure that the
newly introduced canvas has been fully "dipped"
into the painted canvas, then pull the second
canvas off and reveal a whole new piece of art.

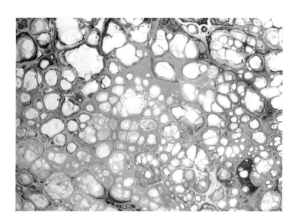

"FuShun" by Rick Cheadle

Negative Space Pour

Another cool technique is a negative space pour.
A negative space pour is basically pouring a
section of the canvas with color and leaving
blank spots "negative space" within or
around the composition.
This creates a visually bold look.

Spin Technique

Place your substrate on a rotating

tray also known as a Lazy Susan.

Then pour paint onto your substrate

while turning or "spinning" the tray.

This produces a swirly effect in the paint.

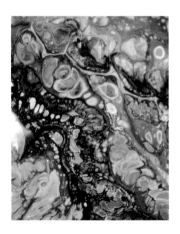

"Stonish" by Rick Cheadle

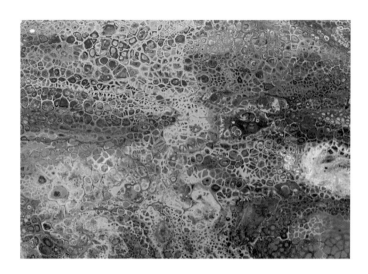

"Timvee" by Rick Cheadle

There are other techniques out there but

the methods listed in this book are the ones I use.

The amount of techniques that can be used are

only limited by your own imagination.

That is why I encourage experimenting as

much as possible.

"Razz" By Rick Cheadle

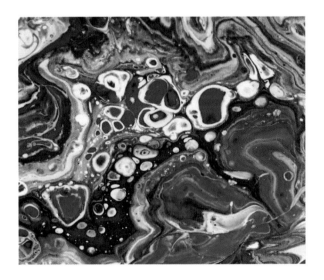

"Blipsy" by Rick Cheadle

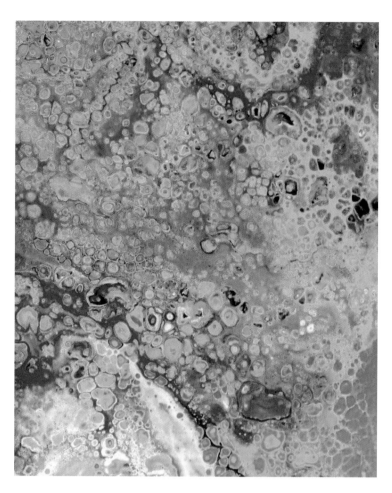

"Pypherso" by Rick Cheadle

Step 5
After The Pour

Drying
I recommend drying your art on a level
surface for 2-3 days before touching it.
There are times that I speed up the drying process
by setting the art outside in direct sunlight,
but that usually causes cracks in the
paint and sometimes I don't want that look.
If you keep your art in an area that is room
temperature to cool, has low humidity
and doesn't get messed with, it should
dry with no issues.

I use this bakery rack that I found at an estate sale
for drying my paint-pouring projects.
Anything will work just so it is in a dust-free
environment and it has a level surface.

Helpful tip - *I use a box and flip it over covering the art to keep dust and insects out of the paint while it's drying.*

Preparing for a protective finish

You may or may not choose to complete your artwork with a finish. Every artist has their own opinion on this. I personally like to have a sheen to my artwork, so I always finish my work with a gloss finish. I also have my pieces finished with resin. I will not delve into the topic of resin in this book but it is a great option to consider.

Helpful Tip - *If you do decide to have a protective finish applied to your piece make sure it is clean! If you used any kind of oil in your paint pouring it is essential to remove it from the surface prior to sealing your work. To remove the oils from the surface you can use talc or corn starch followed by a tack cloth.*

Step 6

Protecting Your Art

Before You Apply Varnish or Resin:

I recommend applying an isolation coat first.
An isolation coat is a layer of medium between
the art and the varnish or resin. It creates a
"separation layer" between the two.
f you are not concerned with being able to
remove varnish 5 - 7 years down the road
you can skip the isolation coat.

While there are several products that can
be used for the isolation coat, my favorite is
GOLDEN℠ Soft Gloss Gel.
Follow the manufacturer's recommendations
when using.

I have listed what I've discovered over the
years to be the pros and cons of varnishing your piece.

Brush-On Varnish

Advantages:

- UV protection
- Stays clean longer
- Evens out the sheen of the work
- Protection from scratches and scuff marks

Disadvantages:

- BRUSH STROKES! In my opinion, this is a major drawback.
- It is hard to get an even coat on large canvases.
- It can totally change the look of a piece, and not always in a good way.

Spray-On Varnish

Advantages:

- ***No Brush Strokes!***
- Stays clean longer.
- Less mess/easy cleanup.
- Evens out the sheen of the work.
- Easier to apply to large substrates.

Disadvantages:

- Fumes require working outdoors or in a well-ventilated area.
- More expensive.
- Dust magnet while drying. Cover carefully.

Step 7
Other Techniques

Embellish with Paint Markers

Add an artistic twist to your piece after it is dry.

"Dream Door" 2017 By Rick Cheadle

This was embellished with paint markers

Dendritic Mono-printing

Place a piece of 8"x12" glass (thrift store picture frame glass will work) under the wire basket that is used for holding your canvas. Do a couple paint pours making sure that the run-off paint lands on the glass.

Once you have enough run-off paint on the glass to cover it, brush the paint covering the glass in one even layer. Then with the same size piece of glass press it into the paint, apply just enough pressure to form a slight seal. (Too much pressure and you could break the glass.) Now release the pressure and see the dendrites! To break the seal, carefully pry the two pieces of glass apart using a sharp knife.

Then take a piece of card stock paper or Yupo paper and lightly press into the paint of one of the glass pieces, carefully pull the paper off and now you have a dendritic monoprint

Helpful Hint: For demonstrations of the mono-printing process, search YouTube 庐 for "Dendritic Mono-Printing"

Using Paint 'Skins'

Things you can make with paint skins:

Mixed media collages.Book covers.
Mosaics. Jewelry. Magnets and More!

Step 8

Selling and Pricing Your Art

Step 1. Set goals.

Do you want to be a full-time artist? Do you want to make enough to pay a few bills a month? Or are you happy just making enough money to buy more paint supplies?

Your aggressiveness in the next steps is

based on your goals. Write them down!

Step 2. Research what is selling.

Go to websites that sell art similar to your style.

Search for top selling items. Are they selling?

Maybe you need to adjust.

Can you produce similar works to what IS selling?

Do your own spin on it and see how it turns out.

Step 3. Show off Your Art!

When you have a large enough portfolio to

showcase, put it out there for the world to see.

This will give you instant feedback on if

you are on the right track...

which leads into the next step.

Step 4. Social Network Presence.

Upload your works as fast as you create them.
The thing to remember is, nobody knows who
you are yet. You have to be OUT THERE.
Pound the pavement. Be a self-promoting machine.
You can be the greatest artist on the
planet but if you're not exposed to the world,
who will even know that you make art?

Step 5. Become part of a community (blogs, social networks, local guilds etc.)

Being connected to like-minded people can
only help you reach your goals.
My mantra when I first started pursuing art
as a full-time profession was,
"Think in terms of NETWORKS
instead of NET WORTH."
The money will come later.
Be a nice person, be helpful, be caring.
And BE REAL!
Don't be phony.
Remember: the more you give,
the more you get.

Suggestions for Where to Sell Your Art:

Galleries
Local stores/gift shops
Arts-and-crafts shows
Flea markets
Consignment shops
Online art markets (Etsy, Inc. and others)
Craigslist, Inc.
eBay, Inc.
Your own Online store
Garage sales
In-house sales/art parties
Arts festivals
Farmers' markets

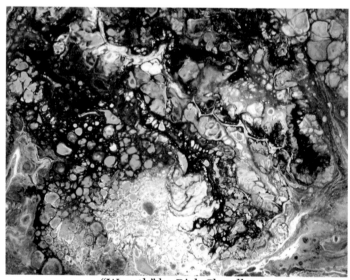

"Wayeth" by Rick Cheadle

Pricing Your Art

Decide what you feel your time and skills are worth.
Do you want to make so much per hour?
Per day? Per week? Once you determine that,
calculate the costs of materials. So, a
sample breakdown would look like this:
I want to be paid $50 per hour for painting,
so if a piece of art takes me an hour or less to
create, I add $50 plus the costs of materials,
let's say $25. So, the price I would charge is $75.
Now, this is a simplistic formula to get you started.
There are other things to consider, but this
is how I did my pricing when I first started
and it worked out fine.

Of course, the more established you
become as an artist the market will begin
to dictate your market value, your art's worth.
Also, supply-and-demand is something to
consider when you reach that level.
For example, if you only release one piece
of art to the public per year, and you are an
in-demand artist, you can charge a premium.

It's all about the market and where you currently fit within that market. The following diagram may be helpful when deciding on how to price your paint pouring art.

Cheadle Designs Art Price Tiers for Paint Pouring Works

Entry Level
Fluid Art Created with "Budget Mix"

$

*Non - Archival
*Recycled Materials Used

Collector
Fluid Art Created with "Fine Art Mix"

$$

*Archival
*Only Quality Materials Used

Fine Art Collector
Fluid Art Created with "Fine Art Mix" and Resin

$$$

*Archival
*Only Quality Materials Used

Please note: Since there currently is no data about the use of silicone or dimethicone as additives in paint pouring, the archival quality of your work cannot be assured when using these ingredients. It is up to you as the artist to decide how address this going forward.

Glossary of Terms

(the way I describe them)

Acetate Sheet – Used for protecting art and transparent mixed media applications. I sometimes use it as a swiping tool.

Analogous Colors – three adjacent colors on the color wheel.

Archival – durability or staying power.

Auto Lubricant – a type of silicone spray that I add to my mix to help produce "cells".

Binder – a substance that holds pigments together.

Bleeding – a dark color seeping into a lighter color.

Blending – joining two colors together with a smooth gradation.

Blooming – a dull, hazy, white effect that occurs on a varnished surface when exposed to moist or humid conditions.

Bookbinders Glue – an archival alternative to use as a pouring medium.

Cells – the cellular designs that are created during the pour.

Coconut milk oil – an additive to help create "cells".

Color Palette – the colors selected to be used in your artwork.

Complementary Colors – opposite colors located on the color wheel.

Consistency -- the fluidity of the paints.

Crazing – the cracked or alligator-skin look on the dried surface of a painting.

Dendritic Monoprint – a type of art created by Squeezing two pieces of glass together (with paint in the middle) then dipping paper on the painted glass surfaces after they are separated.

Dimethicone - an additive to help create "cells". Found in hair and personal lubrication products.

Dirty Pour -- combining two or more paints into a single cup.

Easy Flow™ Panel - cradled rounded-edge paint pouring panel

Flip Cup – the flip cup technique is more of a description of how you get the paint on the surface of your canvas. In short, you flip it over. See details in Chapter#4

Floetrol® -- a paint conditioner. It helps to improve paint flow while maintaining the quality of the paint.

GAC® 800 – a finishing medium used to prevent cracks and crazing. Manufactured by Golden® Art Supplies.

Gesso – artist primer, prepares your substrate for accepting paint.

Gloss Medium – helps increase color intensity, gloss and ease of flowing.

Gloss Varnish -- protects painting with a glossy sheen.

Isolation Coat – a coating that serves as a barrier between the paint surface and varnish.

Knock Down Knife – drywall-finishing tool used for swiping; discussed in Chapter #4

Lacing – the web-like pattern formed in the paint after a pour.

Lightfast – will not fade because of sunlight

Matte Finish – not shiny or glossy; flat.

Mixed-Media – a mixture of techniques, materials and mediums used in an artwork.

Mixology -- the term I use to describe my various mixes.

Monochromatic – tones, tints and shades of one color: tone is color plus black and white; tint is color plus white; shade is color plus black.

Non-Archival – impermanence or unreliable staying power

Opaque – covering up. Unable to see what is underneath.

Pigment – the substance that makes the colors of the paints.

Pipette – a dropper for liquids.

Pouring Medium - colorless paint.

Primary Colors – red, yellow and blue.

Primer – substance applied to substrate to prepare
for painting.

Puddle Pour – the layering colors on the canvas
in one or more puddles that allow the paint to flow
out and or into each other.

PVA Glue – colorless, odorless glue that doesn't break
down over time. An archival alternative to
pouring medium.

Resin – a two-part solution that protects your art with
a glass-like finish.

Secondary Colors – purple, orange and green

Silicone – an additive to help create "cells".
Found in various products like treadmill
lubricant, auto lubricant and others.

Substrate – a surface that paint will be applied to.

Swipe – a technique in which one color is
moved over another color.

Tertiary Color – colors that are achieved by

mixing a primary with a secondary color.
Examples: amber/marigold (yellow–orange),magenta
(red–purple), chartreuse/lime green (yellow–green),
teal/aqua (blue-green), vermilion/cinnabar
(red–orange),and violet (blue–purple).

Transparent – can be seen through; clear.

Translucent – can partially be seen through
(frosted look).

Value – the lightness or darkness of a color.
Example: white is high-value and
black is low-value.

Varnish – a transparent, protective finish.

Yupo® Paper – waterproof and stain-resistant
artist paper.

The Last Word:

The information covered in this book are
the techniques I've developed over the
years in the art world.
These techniques work well for me.
But that doesn't mean it's the only way it
can be done. I am equal parts fan and artist.
I am aware of and in awe of some of my
contemporaries in the paint-pouring world.
I must acknowledge three of them here and now;
search for them on YouTube®.
All three are passionate about their art, about
experimenting and pushing the boundaries,
who can't wait to show the rest of us what
they're learning.

First and foremost is Annemarie Ridderhof,
from Holland. Annemarie is fearless in
her experimentations. Her enthusiasm for this art
form is contagious, and her drive to
share what she learns has garnered her
channel a throng of loyal subscribers.

The second artist I want to mention is
Caren Goodrich, from the United States.
Caren urges her viewers to
"...grab some paint and let's have some fun!"
Caren has been making art for a number
of years and has brought all those skills with her
to channel, *Caren Goodrich.*
When you visit her site, check out her flower
paintings on the back wall of her studio.
Would you believe those were
'painted' with a hammer?!

Deby Coles is another favorite.
(Her channel is Deby at Acrylic Pouring.)
Deby's credo:
*"I promise to share all my paintings,
the failures as well as any successes.
For it is only when we try and fail
that we start to learn."*
Check out her swiping videos,
they are awesome!

If you find another artist's "recipe" that works
better for you, by all means, *use it*!
My way is *not* the only way.
The techniques I covered in this book
are the ones that work for me.
All of the tools and supplies
I have recommended are the actual
tools that I personally use.
But that doesn't mean that they are the only
tools out there. During your research,
you may find other resources to help you
along the way. Follow your creative
spirit wherever it leads you.
What this book covered is basically a
day in the life in my studio.
I didn't hold anything back.
I shared with you everything I know
about paint-pouring that delivers
consistent results for me and my
students and I'm sure they will work for you, too.
But it is up to you to do the work and
apply the techniques...
and most importantly, experiment!
Paint pouring does have a learning curve,
but it is so worth it!

I hope this book pumped you up and got you
excited to go to your studio and
create a masterpiece!
The next step is to put all of the information
in this book to work and start pouring.

If you've enjoyed this book and think
that the information is valuable, please
head over to Amazon, take the time to
share your thoughts, and post a review.
I would greatly appreciate it!

Thank you, and Happy Pouring!

Rick Cheadle
Cheadle Designs LLC
rickcheadle.com

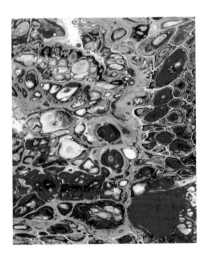

"Fizher" by Rick Cheadle

Please Consider one of my courses on Udemy

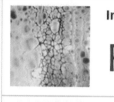

Thank You For Reading

I invite you to share your thoughts and reactions

visit my website

Printed in Poland
by Amazon Fulfillment
Poland Sp. z o.o., Wrocław

50018621R00049